Harmoni
my Hat

Sue Thompson

ISBN: 978-1545419021

British Library Cataloguing in Publication Data.
A CIP catalogue record for this book is available from the British Library.

DEDICATION

For Pete

With thanks for all your help

ACKNOWLEDGMENTS

Front cover: Mike Wilkins

Illustrations:

Pauline Austerfield & Susie Hammond

Suzan Collins: support and direction

Diane Ray: editing and advice.

Jeff Short: for permission to use
Peruvian Boules Rules

Contents

The Beginning

In deepest East Suffolk, close to the windswept beaches of Bawdsey and Shingle Street and just four and a half miles from the market town of Woodbridge, lies a small hidden-away village called Shottisham. Here you will find a picture postcard scene comprising a thatched pub called the Sorrel Horse which dates back to the 15th century, and is owned by a community collective which raised over £400,000 to save it from closure in 2011, and the listed church of St Margaret of Antioch which stands proudly overlooking the village.

Tiny cottages and water meadows complete an idyllic picture. In summer, the loudest sound you will hear is birdsong.

Few tourists venture here, but on a searingly hot, dazzling blue day in July 2006 one tired tourist propped her bicycle against the shaky old white railings that enclose the water meadows, looked around and fell in love. Six years later she was back, this time to stay.

This book is a record of what happened when I followed my instincts, gave up my job and left my family and friends seventy miles away in Essex, and finally, at the age of 62, found where I belonged.

My husband and I didn't move to Shottisham however. We wanted to live in a village with a shop, a pub and a village hall so we bought a house three miles from Shottisham in the village of Hollesley, pronounced Hozelly. Only tourists call it Hollesley, and we weren't tourists any more.

When we first moved here in the summer of 2012, our favourite pastime was to lurk in touristy pubs, glass of red in hand, and wait for a summer visitor to spot our lack of sophistication and air of deep contentment and then, to our infinite delight, ask 'Are you a local?'

Oh yes, we most certainly were!

You'd think our family roots went back 500 years, the way we bored on about the delights of everything in the area, with huge grins plastered over our faces. We felt deeply sorry for the poor unfortunate holidaymakers, who would be departing in a few days to some terrible god-forsaken place like Basildon or Southend (which we smug bastards had just escaped) to work in horrible jobs they couldn't wait to leave. Poor but happy, we were so self-satisfied someone should have locked us up.

Sadly, we have not grown out of this in four years of living here. I long for the summer holidays with the joy that only comes from 60 years of apologising for where I lived. This awful smugness came back to bite me hard in 2015, but I will pluck up the courage to write about this later. Let me give you the good bits first.

We still look around at this beautiful landscape in wonder and then beam at each other and say 'We live here.' Because we do.

We haven't been away from the village for more than four days since we moved here; we might miss something…

Making Friends

In the Crown pub at Snape with friends:
Sue and Danny Bethell
Karrie and Robin Langdon
Christine and Alec Gillespie

The population of Hollesley in 2005 was recorded as 1500, so as the village has grown since then it may now be much higher. It is not a chocolate-box pretty village like Shottisham which I later discovered is made up of around 50% holiday homes, but it is a real place, a working village with a shop and post office combined, a repairing garage, pub, church, village hall, community ground and school.

Many of the people living in and around the village work in the pub, shop or the school and many more are employed at the nearby Hollesley Bay Open Prison. This gives the village a sense of stability and purpose, a real community feeling.

We wanted to become part of this community, so we got into the habit of saying 'Yes' to every invitation that came our way, and four years on we are still doing this wherever possible and the invitations keep pouring in so that even during the long, dark winter months our social lives thrive.

I can recommend this strategy to anyone moving to a small village and perhaps feeling alone and somewhat lost in unfamiliar surroundings. Keep at it! We now enjoy activities we never thought of trying (boules, French Conversation, arts and crafts, more boules) and it has brought us true friendship and great joy.

Our first 'event' was a Fair Trade open house held in the lovely cottage belonging to our new friend Helen, who is an inspiration to everyone in the village, an unstoppable force who cycles long distances for charity, supports the church and works on the council amongst many other worthwhile activities. When my husband suffered a terrifying health scare during our second year in Hollesley, Helen and her good friend Di included us in the prayers said at our local church and I was moved beyond words by this lovely act of simple kindness. The warm glow of acceptance into the community helped us both through a horrible time, giving us much-needed strength and comfort.

At the Fair Trade day we were introduced to many people we now count as friends, and it also brought us into a world that has broadened our circle to include people from Aldeburgh, Thorpeness, Snape, and Leiston. The world of fun and foolery that is the game of boules, or Petanque as it is called in France. We joined the Hollesley boules team, known as The

Bouligans, and up to 10 of us met regularly on Tuesday evenings in the Shepherd and Dog car park to freeze our socks off and hurl our boules willy-nilly in the direction of the cochonet (a small painted wooden ball literally 'little pig' in French) over the rough and pitted tarmac. Aiming is pointless on the whole, you just have to hope to miss the biggest chunks of gravel (and parked cars) and then bomb your opponent's boules into oblivion.

When we first moved into Hollesley Village, in the damp summer of 2012, the houses on our new estate of Swallows Close were still being finished and this meant that we quickly got to bond with our fellow new arrivals. We shared moans about the shortcomings of the builders, the dust and the noise they created and the fact that it seemed to be taking forever to complete the remaining few houses on the estate. We wandered in and out of each other's houses like members of the cast of The Good Life, comparing layouts, room sizes and the quality of each other's bathroom fittings, peering curiously at the various furniture and colour schemes on show, and then our conversations would turn to speculation about the occupants of the newer homes, whom we looked forward to welcoming into the fold. We were the old-timers now, we'd been there at the start. It was like a little club, the first Swallows of Swallows Close.

After a few weeks in our new home we were invited to join the Friday morning coffee club, a gathering of various locals at the pub (where else?) at 11am for coffee, chat, and sometimes homemade cake. We soon came to realise that cake was an indispensable ingredient to accompany any social occasion in the village, and the ability to bake a good one ensured popularity and admiration for the baker. I predict a diet!

Employing our rule of saying 'Yes' to every-thing, we took a deep breath and joined a table of around ten strange faces. All these new people we now count as our friends, and we turn up most Friday mornings to keep up with local gossip. Cakes appear on birthdays, Easter biscuits are baked and mince pies come out at Christmas. It's quite wonderful really.

We join in with everything locally now, and it pays us back in spades. There is a charity quiz which is held on the last Sunday of every month in the Shepherd and Dog, where we quickly formed a team aptly named the Mensa Rejects. We actually won the pot (which is donated to the winning team's charity of choice each month) on our first visit, when we formed a team of eleven. Teams were supposed to be limited to four people but we sort of grew to include several of our neighbours' visiting children who happened to be studying at university, which could explain our never-to–be–repeated success!

The other teams include the Oxleymorons (from the Oxley Dairy holiday villas at Shingle Street), the Sidelights (too dim to be headlights) and the Bouligans, comprising most of our boules team, although they should really be called the Brainiacs as they invariably win. The quiz is set by our illustrious boules captain, Nick Mason, a former teacher, moth expert and sports enthusiast. As we know nothing of moths and loathe all sport, quiz nights are not a highlight of our new life but we didn't come here to show off our intellects (and just as well).

On a happier note, I also joined with several like-minded new friends a village craft club, so wonderful it has its own chapter later. A less successful idea was joining the Parish Council, which I will draw a line under except to say that I soon realised I wasn't cut out for the more confrontational side of village life.

I am now on the Village Hall Committee, where we happily argue about the colour of the stage curtains or what make of hand-dryers to buy. We didn't move here to confront people, we came in peace, and that is just what we have found.

Arts and Crafts

Things I wish I'd done when I was seventeen:

1. Slept with more pop stars - well, ANY pop stars. My best friend's brother Terry from The Avengers, pride of Southend 1965, doesn't count. Oh, and I didn't sleep with him either, he said he didn't fancy me! How could that be?

2. Been nicer to my poor parents. I can't have been much fun, bet they were glad I was an only child.

3. Gone to Art School.

Now that last one really is the Big Regret. How I wish I'd gone to art school. I could have grown my hair down to my bum, stopped shaving my legs and worn Ban-the Bomb T-shirts.

And the boys were, well, the boys were so damned ARTY... and SEXY... and unobtainable, except to other art students, who didn't want them anyway, they were too busy sleeping with pop stars. I really should have gone to art school.

I didn't realise until my mid-fifties that I was in fact an Artiste. I discovered beading along with a love of colour, shape and design.

So when we had been living in Hollesley for about a year I was delighted to find other like-minded people who wanted to craft along with me.

God, how I love craft. I want to adopt Kirstie Allsop and have her permanently sitting at my huge kitchen table making wonderful things out of glue and paper-chains and hemp, waving her perfect nails around and declaring 'Too gorgeous' as she shows off another unidentified glittery object.

We in Hollesley now had our very own Craft Club (oh joy) where we would meet once a month to gleefully make a mess of each other's houses with our sticky creations. We have tried Tunisian crochet, like normal boring crochet except you use huge needles and very thick, colourful wool and your creation grows so fast you could probably crochet Rome in a day. Then came collaging, tea-bag folding and felting. We also have plans to take our talents to the local beaches for a photography workshop, complete with obligatory picnic and sticky buns. There may even be lashings of ginger beer.

All this activity fills me with such joy. Banish your cares with crafting. Don't fret – felt. Don't panic - paint. Keep calm and fold tea-bags! Well, you get the picture.

All this fun with no alcohol, just copious amounts of tea and baked goodies all round.

Of course, crafting has its drawbacks too. We no longer have spare rooms, we have craft workspaces. My poor window ledges all heave with glass painted lanterns, vases, fruit bowls and an Aladdin's cave of beaded jewellery. I can't see a piece of plain glass now without wanting to get the paints out and Art-Deco it up Clarice Cliffe style.

I daren't go near Ikea, although in my dreams I do, I do. There's no hope for me.

One of the many good things about living in the back of beyond, as rude people from Ipswich and Felixstowe call us, is that we lack a good local craft shop to bankrupt us. The Craft Club have been known to travel as far as Tiptree (gasp) to satisfy our craving for craft related stuff, but fortunately distance limits the number of these trips. However, they do provide a great excuse to sample the tea rooms of

Essex, although they're not a patch on Suffolk, of course.

I now look forward to many happy years crafting alongside my messy friends. Long may we cut and paste.

Who'll give me £20 for the Teeth?

If you want to find something quirky and rare (or something manky and broken) and at the same time experience the thrill of the chase or the despair of the loss then you should head into the depths of the Suffolk countryside on a Monday morning, where you will discover the auction rooms at Campsea Ashe.

We were told about this event by one of our coffee morning friends shortly after our arrival in Hollesley, when we were casting about for interesting artefacts to brighten up our dull and featureless new build. Now our bijoux residence is enlivened with oil lamps, paintings, mismatched furniture and dubious kitchenalia from the 1960s (maybe). We have bought lovely mirrors for £2. Three large pictures for £9. We made a present of one of these to an old Essex friend, there really is no end to our generosity. My own personal favourite Campsea purchase was a small bedside table decorated with tiles depicting The Owl and the Pussycat in their boat. Who makes these things? I really would love to know. My grand-daughter, Millie, adores this table and it graces her little bedroom proudly displaying her vast toy cat collection. We hope to live long enough to see it passed on to her own children one day, a priceless family heirloom at a bargain price.

We have become addicted to *Flog It! Antiques Roadshow* and *Put your Money where your Mouth is*. Dangerous things, antiques.

It's the ones that get away that haunt you, the gorgeous mirror some scoundrel outbid you on, seven years bad luck isn't enough for him, the mysterious gadget that I'm sure I could have found a use for if only someone could have told me what it was! I should have bid that extra fiver. Such an addictive guilty pleasure, I look forward to Monday mornings with glee.

It isn't only antiques of course that draw the crowds at Campsea Ashe. There is a wonderful weekly flower, fruit and vegetable sale presided over by the venerable Basil, a spritely chap of ninety-plus who mounts a dangerously rickety platform in the veg shed to call out his wares.

'Who'll give me a parnd for the leeks? Look at 'em, they're good 'uns.'

They're always good 'uns, and who would dare argue with Basil. Not me, that's for sure.

'Well, 80 pee, 70 then. Put 'em away, the buggers don't want 'em. Did you all leave your wallets at home then?'

Some man at the back calls out, 'I'll give you fifty pee.'

It's always some man at the back, it might even be the same man every week, or perhaps there is a team who take turns to batter down poor Basil until he gives in and sells his leeks for fifty pee. And they're good 'uns.

I usually stagger out of Basil's shed with my bag bulging with goodies: tomatoes, leeks, carrots, broccoli, parsnips, and onions. Oh the soups I make with my lovely Campsea stash.

There is an unlovely corrugated iron shed next to Basil's kingdom which is filled with elderly bicycles, rusty lawnmowers and mildewed garden furniture, but this I tend to avoid. I have a terrible suspicion that they auction off dead bodies too, mummified remains of people murdered by Basil in his youth when they tried to buy his leeks for forty pee…

Then we come to the real excitement, the Auction Rooms. Room 2 I call the Posh Room, although this is a relative term. You wouldn't come across Fiona Bruce or Paul Martin here. Instead, the wonderful Geoffrey Barfoot tears through up to 350 items in around two and a half hours. His catch-phrase is 'I won't dwell' and he certainly doesn't. In this huge, cluttered, crowded warehouse you will find boxes of cutlery, whole dinner services, tables, chairs, sofas, pictures and boxes upon boxes of books. All these things and many more on offer, each with its own peculiar, often rather unpleasant smell and each worth a price to someone. But what price? Who will bid highest and secure the prize, and who will go home empty-handed?

By contrast we then come to Room 3, the Tut Room. Some of the stuff on sale in there looks as if it should have been condemned during the Second World War. However, this doesn't stop eager punters crowding in hoping to find that diamond in the rough.

It sometimes puzzles me as to what exactly some of the items on offer in Room 3 actually are, so I wait to be enlightened by the auctioneer. 'A fine example of garden ornamentation.' Really?

'Straight out of house clearance.' Even the auctioneer doesn't know what it is.

And on one memorable occasion; 'Who'll give me twenty pounds for the teeth?'

He held them aloft, they were enormous!

He then identified them as hippopotamus teeth, and as I expect no-one in the room had ever come close enough to a hippopotamus to check out its teeth, no-one attempted to differ. He did get his £20 though. There's a customer for everything at Campsea Ashe, and unfortunately folks, too often it's me.

Llamas on the Piste

Pete and I have never seen the point in sport. Can't stand football (we call it foo-bah), don't understand cricket, what's it all for? We thought we were above all this competitive malarkey, but we were wrong. We have been taken over by a strange, creeping obsession. It's called petanque.

The aim of the game is to throw hollow metal balls (boules) to land as closely as possible to a small wooden ball known as a cochonnet (literally 'piglet') while standing inside a starting circle with both feet together on the ground. The French name comes from 'petanca' deriving from the expression 'pestancats' which means feet together or anchored. A simple enough game but fiendishly addictive.

As mentioned earlier, when we made our move to Suffolk our mantra became

'If asked to join anything, say 'Yes'. So this is how we have ended up hurling boules around the broken-up car park of the Shepherd and Dog on freezing Tuesday nights with several other disturbed villagers with nothing better to do.

Spurred on by our esteemed leader, the well-known quizmaster and birdwatcher of this parish, Nick Mason, we shoot and point in all weathers until darkness drives us into the warmth of the pub, where we huddle together shivering and whimpering, 'Why do we do this, why?' Only alcohol can save us now.

Not content with making fools of ourselves regularly on Tuesday evenings, villagers cross the street to avoid our greetings, tourists point and laugh and take photos on their damn phones, as if playing boules in a car park is a peculiar occupation. Haven't they ever been to France? We have now joined forces with other bouling maniacs from further afield. At the Dolphin in Thorpeness and the Parrot and Punchbowl in Aldringham on alternate Thursdays, as many as thirty boulistes have been known to gather, like a flock of starlings, busily organising themselves into teams and shouting encouragement to each other as they strive to improve their game.

We were invited to join this motley crew by our good friends Reg and Jill whose daughter Debbi is the captain of the Parrot and Punchbowl team. We felt a bit wary at first, thirty noisy boulistes can be a little daunting and several of them seemed quite good! However, we were made very welcome so that now our regular Thursday sessions have become a high spot of the week, in fact we even spent a riotous holiday with twelve of them in France from which we are still recovering. It's very different out there in the wilds where the players have their own rules but won't tell us what they are. I think they cheat, but my French isn't good enough to say so, nor is my courage. I seem to remember that much wine was drunk, which improved my game immensely.

Playing with our new friends has brought us many joys. In fact I can only think of one downside and that is the increase in our waist measurements. Apart from the eat-a-thon that was our trip to France, there is the generosity of the Dolphin and Parrot landlords who regularly offer free food for the hungry players in the much loved form of the cheesy chip. I don't care what the health police have to say on the subject, there is no finer aid to human happiness than the timely appearance, on a cold wet Thursday lunchtime, of large plates of cheesy chips. And mayonnaise. And a large glass of red (unfortunately not free, but hey, we're celebrating here).

During the boules year such events occur as the Mad Hatters Match, which is played out in March, of course, on the pistes opposite the White Lyon in Aldeburgh. You know, the ones next to the beach where the wind howls mercilessly for around 300 days a year. Especially in March. So we hardy boules players don our extravagant millinary creations like a drunken version of Ascot, and try to out-do each other in size and madness of headgear for the prize of a bottle of champagne. This year the winner sported a fine set of peacock feathers on her head. We spent the match ducking from these as they swayed wildly in the gales. They were nearly as long as the lady wearing them was tall. We all needed champagne by the end of the day!

Then there is the annual July jamboree known as Moules and Boules, basically an excuse to get roaring drunk and collapse with heat-stroke at the same venue where you froze half to death in March. You don't have to be mad to play boules, but it certainly does help.

Proof that being a bouliste in our crowd is a truly life-enhancing experience came to us in our second year on the circuit when our good friends Jeff and Jean invited us to their annual charity do, played in their lovely garden in Alderton.

Jeff had constructed a boules piste in a shady corner. Food and unbelievable quantities of alcohol were provided and consumed amidst much singing and cavorting. Even a little boules was played.

Jeff called this magical extravaganza *Peruvian Boules*, with an extremely kitsch carved llama as the prize on offer. It was played strictly by the rules. These are the rules:

1. Gentlemen must wear a hat when mounted.

2. Use of the whip is permitted between consenting adults.

3. Players may not take instruction or guidance from alien life forms during the match.

4. The offside rule. It's a man thing, you wouldn't understand.

5. The basic binary scoring system can be summarized thus: the team with the highest score wins.

6. The Peruvian National Anthem must be sung at the end of every game. We didn't stick to this rule, we just belted out this ditty whenever we felt like it. Rude words were added as the games progressed.

Peruvian National Anthem

Peruvia.......Peruvia

It rhymes with Effluvia

Don't even think of it

We're not in the shit

Peruvia........Peruvia

Nowhere could be groovier

Repeat Ad Nauseum.

(©Jeff Short)

Our games were also enlivened by Jeff and Jean's excitable little Westie, who would wander onto the piste at crucial moments during play, to drunken cries of 'Llama on the Piste! '

This has become our catch phrase now, so if anyone should stand in the way of play, some wag will shout 'Llama on the Piste!' to the bewilderment of the non-bouling public. We don't bother to explain. They wouldn't understand.

Harmonicas

Round my Hat

If you go down to a pub round here you might get a nice surprise. Or a nasty shock. It all depends on your attitude to live music, or more especially live folk music. Arrghh - the real thing; sea shanties and bawdy ballads; tragic stuff about stabbings, shootings and incest, all served up with Suffolk swagger, or stagger as the evening and the alcoholic intake of the performers progresses.

I have to confess here that Pete and I have a long-held love of all things folky having met at the end of the sixties when such music was much more highly regarded than it is now. We would frequent our local Folk Club, a smoky dive above the Railway Hotel in Southend where the corners were dark and the beards were long. We wore our cord trousers and kaftans with pride, bells on our shoes and beads round our necks. Really, I'm not making this up. We recently showed the photos to our children and they said it was grounds for adoption. This behaviour would get you arrested or beaten up now, but probably not in Suffolk.

Our lovely local hostelry, the Sorrel Horse in Shottisham, hosts a music evening every month which we usually manage to attend. We have enjoyed many varied acts ranging from folk/jazz to a wonderful family known as Ross Burkitt and Eliza, being a very talented father and daughter occasionally accompanied by the equally talented Alison, Eliza's proud mother. Eliza is now fifteen, and she sings and plays the violin so beautifully that people travel long distances for the pleasure of seeing her. She recently gave a recital in our local church in order to practise her music college entry audition before an audience and it was one of the most moving occasions I've had the pleasure to witness. This sort of thing seems to happen around here all the time, and I am so proud and grateful to be part of it.

The musicians at the folk nights play at one end of the Sorrel's tiny dining room, while we the audience are crammed into the remaining space as best we can. Latecomers perch perilously close to the fire at the back of the pub, a popular spot in winter but the flagstones can be mighty cold on the bum during the summer months when the fire remains unlit. We cheat and take our own folding chairs, a shameful sign of advancing years but it gives a smug satisfaction as others of similar vintage attempt, sometimes successfully, to sit on the floor. Watching them attempt to get up again can be more entertaining than watching the bands.

My favourite event at the Sorrel Horse so far has to have been the riotous Penny Gaff Evening. Penny Gaff was a series of short theatrical entertainments for the lower classes in 19th Century England, traditionally held in the back room of a public house, so admirably suited to revival at the Sorrel. It was said to consist of a variety of performers with the emphasis on humour so we should expect comic songs, sketches and bawdy stories. We were not disappointed.

Various characters from different parts of Suffolk ranging from Ipswich to Knodishall gave us an evening of mad, hilarious turns, including a man who wrote his own doggerel (what a great word that is). Apparently he tours village halls giving his performances and is in great demand. He proceeded to deliver Stanley Holloway's Albert and the Lion. You remember the one where the little boy is eaten by the lion at Blackpool after poking it with a stick with the 'orses 'ead 'andle, and after they'd paid to get in. The doggerel man had of course added his own embellishments, and very droll they were too.

Next was a sombre recital of 'The Pig', an Irish poem about the pitfalls of the demon drink, which I fondly remember my Dad performing after partaking too much of the demon drink himself. It is a much-loved childhood memory, and I had to restrain myself from joining in. I also remember Dad performing Albert and the Lion while in his cups, so it was no wonder I felt so at home!

Anyway, back to 'The Pig'. This piece should ideally be delivered in a slow, lugubrious manner; a slightly slurred voice and gentle alcoholic sway always adds to the impact, too. Here it is, in all its mournful glory.

The Pig

Twas at the end of last November, or as near as I remember

I was walking down the street in drunken pride

With a stumble and a stutter

I fell into the gutter

And a pig walked up and lay down by my side

As I lay there in the gutter

Not a murmur or a mutter

A lady passing by was heard to say

You can tell a man who boozes

By the company he chooses

And the pig got up and slowly walked away.

Audience, in sorrowful refrain,

He walked a waaaaaayyy...

This is a cue to wipe a tear from your eye and head for the bar. There may be a bit of a scramble.

Back in the sixties, Pete was very briefly in a band which at a stretch could be described as 'folk' (this is one of the reasons I married him, the other being that he had a car!). He also came from a large family, many of whom also played musical instruments. For an only child from a quiet home this was very heaven, and it was hard for his poor parents to persuade me to go home at all.

Pete's band (I don't recall their name, probably something like Pete, Paul and Janet, this being the sixties, that great era of inventive band names) would meet for practise several times a week, usually in his long-suffering parents' living room. They went out a lot. When I had been on the scene for a few months and had been accepted as part of the gang, some fool asked if I could sing. Well, pass the party seven and we'll give it a go, shall we? I know all the words.

We decided my maiden performance would be *Donna, Donna*. This was a truly terrible song, originally sung by Pete, Paul and Mary. It was quiet, plaintive, and mercifully short, and was well deserving of the fate it met at my hands. I cringe now to think that I imagined people actually enjoyed listening to me. They were kind and didn't boo or throw things. But they didn't clap either, so I took the hint after a while and reverted to my role of admiring (silent) band follower. Best all round, really.

But sometimes, on open mic nights in the Sorrel, I dream of walking onto the improvised stage, closing my eyes and, to a hushed and adoring crowd, reliving my glory days once more...2, 3, 4... *Donna, Donna, Donna, Donnaaaaa...*

In a little village called Blaxhall, around two miles deep into the countryside surrounding Snape, you will find another magical musical pub called the Blaxhall Ship. This pub oozes atmosphere. It is hot, cramped, noisy, crowded, all the ideal requirements for a folky experience to savour. You never know what you are going to get. We love to just rock up on our way to or from somewhere else, to see what's occurring. We have come across a very bawdy elderly lady, who sang a very bawdy elderly song, the words of which I could not believe at the time, and which I have since mercifully forgotten. The Sorrel crowd would have loved her!

People tend to dance at the Blaxhall Ship, which is brave as often there is scarcely room to stand. It makes fetching a round from the bar somewhat daunting. Likewise trips to the loo. The dancing is often not connected to the music at all, but I think this is just the Suffolk way. Folk tend to have their own interpretation of things around here.

One memorable afternoon we brought two of our old Essex friends to share the Blaxhall Ship experience. It was that very rare and wonderful thing, a hot Bank Holiday weekend, and the place was rammed. We perched on uncomfortable chairs outside with a noisy crowd of Suffolk reprobates who had probably been propping up the bar for most of August. We were in for a treat.

Amongst our Tuesday car park boules players is a talented musician from Bawdsey by the name of John. We never could remember his surname, so we hit on the catchy nickname of 'Bawdsey John'. Just for the hell of it. John played the harmonica, and sometimes the guitar, in a local band called *Faites Accompli*. They would turn up in all sorts of places: fetes, pubs, village halls etc, with their lively interpretations of folk music, blues, skiffle, rock and roll. A glorious mix of enthusiastic roistering that was guaranteed to please a crowd. As luck would have it, they were playing that day for us at the Blaxhall Ship!

I was especially pleased on that day as John seemed to have brought his entire collection of harmonicas along. Now, I always enjoy a harmonica in a band. It gives a Bob Dylan vibe that takes me back to the good old Railway Hotel days whenever I hear one played. We settled down, drinks and crisps to hand, in gleeful anticipation.

The highlight of the afternoon was *Faites Accompli's* bluesy rendition of that good old favourite, *My Old Man's a Dustman* to the tune of the Stones famous *Little Red Rooster*....

Oh, my old man's a dustman...da Daaa da da da da

He wears...a dustman's hat...da Da, de da da da da

The well-oiled audience, including ourselves, joined in with gusto. It was an unforgettable experience, with Bawdsey John centre stage with his harmonicas, which he had placed around the rim of his battered old hat to enable him to change instruments during a song without having to get out of his chair. Genius.

Our Essex friends were very impressed. Well, John is a handsome lad and a harmonica solo to accompany *My Old Man's a Dustman* on a sun drenched Bank Holiday Monday outside a country pub is an occasion to be cherished.

Thirty Eight Days

in Summer

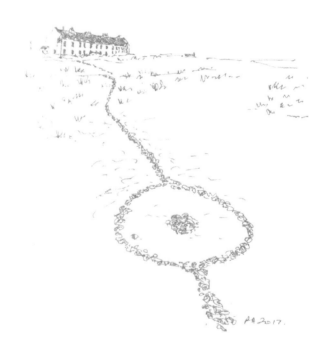

This is the chapter which I have dreaded writing since starting this book. Where the fun stops and it all gets serious. No hippopotamus teeth or llamas on the piste, no silly songs or bawdy stories. It's the event I hinted at in chapter one when I said that my smugness would come back to bite me but it wasn't me who got bitten, it was my lovely man.

It was Thursday, July 23, 2015. A quiet, warm, windless day. So normal. Our daughter had gone with her family to the Isle of Wight, camping with friends, leaving their little dog Poppy in our care. The first week of the long summer holidays, when the tourists flock in and the camp sites fill up, our last day of boules at the Dolphin before the crowds push us out of the pub garden and we have to move to the larger space at the Parrot and Punchbowl for the summer.

We decided to take Poppy along, and all our dog-loving boules friends made a fuss of her. So did their dogs. We had a few games, then sat happily chatting and eating cheesy chips in the sunshine. I'm so glad we did this, because I think it is my last totally carefree happy memory. I look back on the relaxed, innocent person I was then and wish I could go back and find her. I miss her.

After another hour's boules, Pete and I discussed having a light lunch in Thorpeness but then decided that as we had Poppy with us we would take her home and carry on to Martlesham to do the dreaded big shop. Pete said he felt a little tired.

After our shop, we loaded the heavy bags into the car. Pete lifted the ones containing the large bottles of water. He seemed to find this a bit of a struggle, and I remember feeling uneasy.

We drove home, some of the heat had gone out of the day and the air felt soft, gentle. A quiet time, waiting for something to happen.

Arriving home, we carried in the heavy bags and unpacked. It was 5pm. Pete put on the TV and sat down to watch *Pointless* while I prepared a chicken salad. *Pointless* finished, and the news began. I started to dish up our meal and as I did Pete said, 'I really don't feel well, pass me my antacid pills.'

I handed him the bottle of pills, with a glass of water. He pushed up the lid, the pills flew up in the air and Pete said, 'Help me, I'm going to fall.' Before I could even reach him he fell onto the floor, face grey, lips purple, and he just stopped breathing. My husband was lying lifeless on the floor and I was alone except for the bloody dog that was jumping over Pete's body, barking madly. The television blared, I couldn't work out how to turn it off.

I managed to get the back door open, throw poor Poppy into the garden and turn off the television, then picked up my phone to call for help. But we are miles from anywhere. We have a first response team but I didn't know their number and, anyway, my fingers wouldn't work to use the phone. My husband was dying and I was completely useless.

Then instinct kicked in. I realised Pete needed CPR immediately and I remembered we had a couple of neighbours who were police officers and would be trained in CPR. They had young children so surely one of them would be at home. Leaving my front door wide open, I ran to their house and banged madly on their door. I was actually screaming 'Help' as well. People really do that Hayley opened the door, with her children round her looking scared, as well they might. 'My husband's collapsed,' I shouted. 'Help me.'

Then I started to cry. Hayley and her partner Simon left the children with their neighbours, Liz and Niall, and they both ran into our house where Simon started CPR while Hayley rang the paramedics. They continued to take turns to breathe into him and attempt to restart his heart for 20 minutes, but they were exhausted by then.

This is when my wonderful friend Liz had the idea of calling in another neighbour, Keith, who was in the merchant navy and knew how to perform life-saving procedures. Keith took over from Simon and Hayley, and this time Pete actually started breathing again, but only for a few moments.

By this time the paramedics had arrived, and they used a defibrillator to shock his heart into beating. I think they did this three times and each time he would breathe for a while then stop again. I watched in disbelief. How had this happened without warning, would he survive? I clung to Liz, feeling useless and stupid. I just didn't know what to do.

Poor Poppy was still barking fit to bust in the garden, and small knots of neighbours had gathered all down the close like carnival spectators – an air ambulance had been called and Liz found the key-holder for our community grounds so that the ambulance could take Pete around to where it had landed as soon as they had stabilised him. This seemed to take forever, as he was fitted with tubes to help him breathe while they flew him to Basildon.

All the time the bloody sun shone, the dog barked, and I shook with fear and shock. The paramedics stretchered my husband into the ambulance; there wasn't room for me to go with him even to the air ambulance due to the amount of equipment needed to keep him alive so I just held his hand as they took him through the door and then I stumbled back into my crowded house. I went to thank Simon and Hayley and Keith but they all looked grim.

Hayley said, 'It isn't good,' and started crying. 'He was down for more than half an hour. He's very ill.' She knew from her training that people who were deprived of oxygen for long periods often didn't survive or had severe brain damage. She didn't tell me this, for which I am so grateful. What I also didn't know was that Pete had suffered a cardiac arrest, which has a survival rate of around one in four.

Pete was taken by air ambulance to Basildon Cardiac Unit, rather than Papworth, as then I could stay nearby with my son in Rayleigh and have the support of my family through what was to come. It was now becoming dark and as I have poor night vision, Liz and Niall drove me to Basildon. These wonderful friends drove 150 miles, just dropping me off then turning straight back through the horrible rush hour traffic on the A12. Niall had already done a full days' work and hadn't eaten either. They wouldn't take any money for petrol, just said, 'Give him our love.' and drove off.

I'll always remember the kindness we were shown that day. It kept me sane throughout the long and frightening weeks ahead. Our village saved my husband's life and then they supported me and prayed for us through the darkest of times because they are good people.

When I was taken to the cardiac unit, my son was already in the family room. Pete's temperature had been reduced to stop further damage to his brain, and the doctors told us he would remain in an induced coma for three days then they would slowly raise his temperature to bring him round again. What they told my son but mercifully didn't tell me was that it was likely that Pete would not survive the first night.

The next three days were spent either sitting with Pete in the hospital or lying sleepless in my little grandson's bed, texting my friends through the endless nights. I still have these texts on my phone, they were so powerful and inspiring to me when I needed a hand to hold in the early hours of the morning. The message I treasure the most is from my fellow crafter, Karrie, dated 24th July when I was probably at my most terrified. 'He will be ok. Remember all the things you planned to do together. Remind him of your plans. He will be there with you to enjoy it.'

On the 25th, the day before he was due to be brought out of the coma and I felt so bad because I couldn't reach him, Karrie texted, at 6.44am, 'I believe that they know you are there 'cos they can feel your love.'

When Alister, my son, and I went up to the hospital that morning we were told that they were starting to wake him up and that by around 2pm he should show signs of consciousness. The nurses then needed to get a reaction from him before switching off the machine controlling his breathing, and enabling his body to function independently.

We squeezed his poor fingers, Alister and I, whispering, 'Wake up, wake up.' He didn't. We tried to get him to move his toes, with no reaction. After about an hour he made a small response, the toes waggled, the fingers curled and at last the nurses acknowledged that he was coming out of the coma and could now breathe unaided. This was such a huge relief. I thought he would sit up and start talking to us within minutes but in fact it would be more than two days before he spoke and many more before we knew the results of the MRI scans which would confirm whether or not he had sustained brain damage.

On the same day, a young woman on Pete's ward was awoken from an induced coma and pronounced brain dead. We sat in the family room as far away from her weeping family as we could get.

Quietly, we left the hospital and prepared for another sleepless night while awaiting developments. My poor son looked shattered, he and his family should have been enjoying a week in Scotland but instead we were trying to comfort each other while keeping up an air of normality in front of the children.

That evening, I was sitting mindlessly watching the television, *Top Gear,* my grandsons favourite apparently, not that I had noticed, and my fourteen year old granddaughter Evie did a lovely thing. She told me she had run me a bath and I could help myself to her precious Lush bath products. The ones we had chosen on a girlie trip to Ipswich earlier in the year, in another, happier, life. So I created a scented sanctuary for myself and had a much needed cry in private.

The following day it was back to the hospital, no change still. Pete had been put in a high dependency ward, Roding, while MRI scans were done to assess any damage to his brain. He still had no speech and showed no sign of knowing who we were.

The next day, 28th July, we took in some family photos to see if he recognised anyone and if this would bring back any speech. He had some of the tubes removed by now, and seemed more peaceful. As I bent down to show him the photos he looked at me and said very clearly 'Hello'. Oh, wow!! Until now I'd thought he may never speak again, the joy I felt was overpowering. I actually had hope.

Things then became slowly better for a while, Pete regained much of his mobility and while still asleep most of the time, he responded to our visits and seemed to know what was going on around him, but I didn't want to get too hopeful until the MRI scan results came back. These were scheduled for Thursday 30th, so after another sleepless night I went to Hyde Hall with my grandchildren to take my mind off what was to come.

Of course, it was a lovely hot summer's day, beautiful gardens and an Alice in Wonderland trail for the children to follow. My lovely daughter in law, Sarah, bought me chocolate cake and we all sat in the pretty cafe with our party type food which I crumbled and pushed around before passing it to the grandchildren. I couldn't eat for shaking, all I could think was what will I do if his brain is damaged, how will we all cope. I watched my happy little grandchildren and wondered how I would break bad news to them if bad news came. But most of all I checked the time constantly. I wanted this day to be over.

That evening we went to the hospital mob-handed, myself, Alister, Helen and her husband, Phil. I needed people to physically push me into the ward, the impulse to run away and hide was so strong. When the doctor came the first thing I thought was that he looked too young to bring such important news, we needed the head honcho in a suit and tie looking solemn, but this lovely guy was so relaxed and matter of fact and he gave me the news I had been too scared to hope for. No brain damage, the scan was normal! I played this scene back in my head over and over in the difficult weeks to come. Normal, my new favourite word.

We all floated onto the ward beaming like idiots. Helen said, 'Isn't this cool, us all being here together?' And it was - so, so happy.

Pete stayed at Basildon until August 6th and then he was moved to Ipswich hospital where the experts in neurosurgery could work on his speech and word recognition. He had all sorts of problems with understanding what objects were and also with memory and spatial awareness. I was told this was part of the recovery process and hopefully he would regain all his former abilities, but this wasn't guaranteed to happen. Pete was upset and frustrated because he couldn't tell the time or add up. He also had problems reading and his writing was extremely poor. I realised he had a long, hard struggle ahead but I was determined to help in any way I could.

Things improved slowly and I was told that Pete may be fitted with a defibrillator before coming home so that if he had another cardiac arrest the machine would restart his heart. I don't want him to come home before this is done because I would be too scared to leave him in case it happened again. However, the defibrillator will not be fitted until the doctors feel that his quality of life is good enough to merit the cost of fitting one, and this is where we hit our next hurdle. Unfortunately, Pete had been fitted with a catheter in the hospital and this had caused him to develop a urinary infection. The pain and distress this caused led him to become confused and upset, and this led to a very bad experience indeed.

It was Sunday, August 9th. I didn't know this at the time but weekends are always more difficult because the ward tends to be understaffed. When I arrived Pete was rambling and incoherent, clinging to me and saying he wanted to go home. I couldn't find anyone to tell me what was going on, but I realised the problem was to do with the catheter. It was all he could focus on, and the doctors chose that day to do the neurology test to see if he merited a defibrillator. They asked him who the prime minister was and the president of the USA but all he talked about was the pain caused by the catheter, he didn't understand why they were asking what seemed to him to be stupid questions. I tried to explain to the doctors that he had an infection and wasn't feeling well but they seemed too rushed to listen. One of them then said he didn't think a defibrillator was called for as Pete's quality of life didn't merit one. It felt like a slap in the face.

That evening was in fact my lowest point.

Too exhausted to care about my pride any more, I rang my son and just sobbed over the phone that I'd had enough and couldn't go on. I still feel ashamed of this, I'd tried not to be a burden on the family but the fear and lack of sleep had worn me down and now all my hope had gone. Unable to stand being in the house on my own any more, I put my sunglasses on and walked into the village.

This was that beautiful time of year when the village looks at its loveliest. It was 7pm, no-one was about, just me and the birds and the golden sunshine. I walked past all the places where Pete and I had been so happy and I mentally said goodbye to it all, the pub where we had thrown our boules in all weathers, Karrie's thatched cottage where the craft club had met, the school where I had briefly worked as a dinner lady, the community garden where we had gathered to sing hymns at the harvest festival. Every step drenched in memories that would now be just that, because I had decided to sell the house and return to my family in Essex.

Exhausted, I knew I couldn't cope alone.

I walked right to the end of the village to the caravan site at Run Cottage, where we had first discovered Hollesley all those years ago. I turned right up Bushey Lane towards the Sorrel Horse and remembered the folk nights, the Penny Gaffe, and lovely summer evenings drinking with our friends. I said goodbye to living here and all the things I'd come to love.

I walked, I cried.

Well, you'll be pleased to hear, if you've borne with me so far, that this was as far as the self-pity went because the next day I woke up feeling much more positive and in fact I was ready for a fight. After all, I still had plenty worth fighting for!

There's nothing like a spot of shopping for cheering a girl up, so I went into Woodbridge and bought Pete a razor. Not one of your flimsy disposable excuses for a razor, but a proper one in a box, with instructions even. Rock and roll!! My reward for this piece of generosity was a phone call from the hospital. It was my man on the hospital phone and he said, normal as you like 'Hey, Sue, did I have a heart attack?' He remembered everything! I explained what had happened without too many gory details, and he was amazed. He kept saying, 'Did I really have a cardiac arrest?' as if it was some kind of Olympic achievement. He just couldn't believe it, which I could understand because I didn't really believe it either. Big scary stuff like this doesn't happen to little frivolous people like us.

When I arrived at the hospital, new razor in hand, Pete showed no signs of distress or confusion. Helen had also come to visit, so there was a bit of a party atmosphere which was lifted even higher when the neurologist came to carry out more tests and this time Pete gave them all the right answers in the right order. He now qualified for the defibrillator which would be fitted at Basildon as soon as possible.

There followed a very frustrating week during which Pete's mood swung from hopeful to depressed but finally, on August 23rd, he was taken back by ambulance to Basildon for the operation to be carried out.

However, fate had one final arrow left to fling at him still.

On the morning of August 24^{th,} Alister and I arrived at the ward expecting to wish the patient luck for his operation, but instead we found him in tears. It had been discovered that the urinary infection was still present in his system and the operation was cancelled. A shame this could not have been confirmed before Pete was prepped and gowned ready to be taken into theatre, with all the anxiety and hope this entailed. The worst part was that now he may have to wait another two weeks for the operation to be performed.

No wonder he was in tears.

We stayed with Pete for the rest of the day, trying to keep his spirits up, although the two of us were by now exhausted and close to tears ourselves.

My daughter Helen arrived in the evening so we left her with her father and went back to Alister's house to eat and take a rest, and then we had a call from Helen. The infection had cleared up and the operation could be carried out that week. Stop the roller-coaster, we want to get off!

Finally, at 2pm on Wednesday 26th, a successful operation was carried out and my husband is now the proud owner of his own personal defibrillator. It is about the size of a match box and makes for an interesting body feature as it sits raised from his chest and at the moment is a fetching shade of yellow tinged with black. We are told this will improve with wear. Can't wait.

The patient was in a lot of pain and dosed heavily with painkillers, but he was very, very happy. He kept saying 'I'm normal '.

For some reason this made me cry.

The wonderful doctors gave us lots of information on what had been done and why and what to expect in the coming weeks. We were from the start treated with great respect and compassion, never made to feel stupid or in the way with our constant questions and anxieties.

Pete returned to Ipswich hospital the next day and at last I was home for good. I celebrated with more shopping, this time for presents for Liz and Karrie, who had been such true friends to me when I needed it most.

Pete was back in Sproughton ward for two days before being discharged to come home.

On Saturday 29th August, a hot and perfect Bank Holiday weekend, I filled the car with petrol, did a huge food shop to refill my bare cupboards then collected Liz who had agreed to drive me to the hospital to help with all Pete's pills and general luggage so that I could sit in the back holding his hand, and we went to collect my man.

At around 12.30 he staggered unsurely from the car, exhausted. He had been sitting on his hospital bed waiting for me since 5am as he was scared that I wouldn't come and he would have to stay in hospital. He's afraid of everything, the bed, the neighbours, the house, everything is just too much for him.

That first night was truly terrifying as Pete got up at 3am and insisted on shaving and trying to cut his hair. He keeps forgetting that he has taken his pills and tries to take them again. I feel that I can't cope with him but I have to. I wish I had some help, but my family are now seventy miles away and I don't want our friends to see him like this, it would distress him too much.

In the end I rang Helen and also Pete's sister Christine and her husband Mike. They all turned up with the grandchildren and Poppy the puppy, and this turned out to be the best thing I could have done as it cheered him up and made everything seem normal. I think my panic was probably rubbing off on him, I had to calm down and stop babying him. I wasn't his mum!

On the last day of August I did what I'd been dreaming of doing since that terrible event on July 23rd, I went with my husband for a walk along Shingle Street. This is our very special place, a place of hope and healing, and as I watched him walking with our visiting son, smiling and chatting like he used to,

I finally felt I had my husband back. Thirty eight horrible days and now it was finally over.

Where Everyone Knows

My Name

So that's all the drama out of the way.

There followed a very strange, eerie few months when we pretended everything was as it had been before, tip-toeing carefully around each other being unnaturally polite, afraid to act normally because being normal was something we felt we had lost, as if we somehow didn't deserve it.

We took to sleeping in separate rooms, after more than forty years of cheerfully cosying up together at night. I would lie in my lonely bed listening to Pete snoring, it became my favourite sound. If I couldn't locate any noise to reassure me he was still breathing, I would creep into his room and listen until he grunted or moved, then I would return to my lair again, reassured that I wouldn't be bothering the neighbours that night. I had done this kind of thing forty years earlier when my son was a baby, prodding the poor child's chest until he moved or cried so that I knew he was still alive and I could go back to sleep safe in the knowledge that my little family was ok. Understandable in a nervous new first –time mother, not such desirable behaviour from a wife.

On the few occasions when sleeplessness led me to actually climb into bed beside my husband, I would lie as far away from him as I could get without falling out of bed and remain motionless for fear of disturbing him. It didn't really help the sleeplessness but it did comfort me and hopefully him too.

As Pete's driving licence had been revoked until the authorities deemed him fit to drive again, a long and depressing process which we were promised would take six months but in the end dominated our lives for more than nine, I was promoted to family chauffeur.

To say that I don't like driving is like saying that Donald Trump doesn't like Hilary Clinton. I finally passed my driving test on the fifth attempt, at the age of 42 (it's the meaning of Life, the Universe and everything, you know) having first attempted lessons aged 22 and being forced to give up for financial reasons when I left work to have my first baby. This was a huge relief both to myself and my poor instructor. I only took up driving lessons again when my Dad died suddenly and we inherited his new car. Mum couldn't drive and it was pass my test or go with her everywhere on the bus. When the instructor told me I had passed my reaction was 'I don't believe you '.

The first time I drove on my own I was so terrified I was tempted to close my eyes when overtaking.

So you can imagine my delight when I found myself forced to brave the A12 run to my family in deepest Essex, home of the container lorry and the maniacal towie drivers. I know that if I were to take my eyes off the road for even a nanosecond a container lorry big enough to contain a small continent would pounce on me and crush my poor Kia Picanto into sub-atomic particles.

Then there were our own local roads, or goat tracks if you want to be accurate. Infested with giant tractors driven by escaped felons from Hollesley prison, and home to the lycra lout brigade of cyclists who will only venture out if they can ride 14 abreast at 13 miles an hour. Oh boy!

Add to this the fact that I have such limited night vision I have been known to walk into walls at night, while completely sober, and you can see how interesting my life became during this time. I lived in a state of permanent fear, which only eased slightly towards the end of my chauffeuring stint. When Pete's licence was finally returned I partied like it was 1999. It was tempting never to get into the driving seat again, but my bullying friends and family insisted that I 'keep my hand in' so I trundle to Campsea Ashe on a Monday and boules on a Thursday, dodging the lycra hordes and whistling a happy tune.

We have been welcomed back with great enthusiasm into the Thursday boules fraternity. Shortly after Pete's return from the hospital, on 26th September, Jeff and Jean of 'Llamas on the Piste' fame asked us to join them for a meal at the Parrot and Punchbowl to celebrate our wedding anniversary (we share the same date with them). It was a lovely warm day so the four of us sat in the pub garden and enjoyed a delicious meal and a bottle of prosecco which was kindly given to us as a present by our friend Sheila Fleming, the landlady and provider of fabulous cheesy chips. We were very happy.

For a while, Pete had the kid-gloves treatment from people who seemed unable to believe he was still there, so it was a great relief when they resumed teasing and ribbing him as they do all the other players.

This was demonstrated all too enthusiastically recently when, during a particularly poor run of shots, one of the players suggested that the best thing Pete could do to improve his team's chances was to make a visit to the toilet!

This has now become another of our boules catch-phrases, along with 'You can put your own score up, then' when a team humiliates their opponents with a crushing defeat and then gloats. No-one loves a gloater.

We are now 16 months on from The Event, as we now refer to Pete's exciting medical history. This was the actual phrase used by the knee specialist at Ipswich hospital when Pete went to see if he was suitable for a knee replacement. The guy took one look at his medical notes, backed away a little and refused to recommend anything more dangerous than deep heat rub. Apparently they would have to turn his defibrillator off to give him a general anaesthetic. At this point I added deep heat rub to the shopping list. But life here in Suffolk goes merrily on ... Some things have been lost. Basil retired recently and vegetables are no longer auctioned at Campsea Ashe. You can buy them from a small shed at a very reasonable price, but there is no haggling allowed so where's the fun in that?

The craft club is no more, it just wasn't possible to find a time when everyone was free so now I cut and paste alone, messing up my own house instead of Karrie's.

We no longer play boules in the car park of the Shepherd and Dog after a memorable evening when, unbeknown to us, the Dog had booked a music study evening for the U3A and a large woman in a large 4x4 parked on the piste while a game was in progress. Nick approached her (I wish I'd thought to get a picture) and politely asked her to move as we were trying to play a game. U3A lady (I think her name was Boudicca) then squared up to him and informed him in booming tones that it was a pub car park and as a customer she was entitled to park there. Honestly, some people!

The Sorrel Horse has now built a piste for us behind the pub, so we drive to Shottisham for games on a Tuesday, but I miss the good old days battling with the pot-holed piste at the Dog. It brought a new meaning to the phrase 'pot luck', and it was easier to duck into the pub when rain stopped play.

One thing that has not changed though is our obsession with the Suffolk folk scene. When Pete regained his driving licence in April we started to venture further afield and discovered Folk at the Froize Inn. This wonderful restaurant in Chillesford, with its huge grounds and delicious food served from outdoor catering vans and its marquees and fires, became our own mini Glastonbury. The owner of the Froize also booked

Leiston theatre for a one-off folk evening, opened up a pop-up bar and took along some delicious nibbles. They booked a brilliant band called Merry Hell who kept us all entertained on a cold wet October evening.

The place was packed, Suffolk folk at its best.

Also playing at this event were our new favourites, a very popular duo on the folk circuit called the Broadside Boys. We had seen them previously at the Sorrel Horse and they made a huge impression on me because their songs could have been written for us. The Broadside Boys come from Little Glemham near Stratford St Andrew, a very lovely rural spot which we visit often as a few of our boules friends also live there. But the songs they write cover the whole of our beloved corner of Suffolk, Aldeburgh, Southwold, Thorpeness and, of course, Shingle Street, which is only 2 miles from where we live. When I first heard them sing 'Moving to the Country', I wanted to stand up and cheer as it conveys exactly how I feel about our great adventure.

However, my personal favourite song is called 'Where everyone knows my name', our very own anthem for our new home. It describes all the sophisticated, exotic places people love to visit on holiday, New York, Paris etc, but on returning we are where we really want to be, where we belong.

Where everyone knows my name

Give me a bar stool

Give me an open fire

Give me a good friend

And time to talk awhile

There is a path, there is a road

That takes me back to where I
want to go

A village green

A little lane

A place I go where everyone
knows my name.

Some people have suggested that we bring our own instruments and join in when jam sessions are held at places like the Blaxhall Ship or the Swan at Alderton, and I must admit it is tempting to give it a go. How hard can it be?

The man himself has even hinted that this year's Christmas list should include such items as a harmonica, a ukulele and Bert Weedon's *Play in a Day*. I remember the latter very fondly, I even had my own battered copy once from which I learned to play 'Bobby Shaftoe'.

I am sure this would go down well at the Blaxhall Busk, or at least it would give the other musicians something to laugh at during the long, dark Suffolk winter evenings. We do love a good laugh along with the more gloomy songs beloved of folk aficionados and our good friend, Bluesy Ray Booth, from the boules crowd provides much merriment for us with his witty performances. Strumming his ukulele (this is where Pete got the idea) and with a mournful expression worthy of a basset hound, Ray gives us his version of 'I Don't Look Good Naked Any More' with the Blaxhall crowd joining in with gusto. Look it up on YouTube and I guarantee you'll be singing it all week.

While you're there take a look at 'Girl from the Fens' too, another of Ray's gems - goes down a treat with a pint and a curry on a Thursday night.

Huddling in Hollesley

In the deep midwinter it can be hard to prise a Suffolk villager from their comfy home. Winkling the inhabitants of Hollesley out into the freezing wind that blows off Shingle Street on a dark December night can be a challenge, especially on a Saturday night when Strictly beckons. Huddling becomes a village sport.

However, gatherings have been known to occur between the usual suspects:

Nick, Ray, Gill, Karrie, Robin, Pete and myself. We pick a night, choose a venue, and start planning. Cakes are baked and lovingly wrapped, fizzy drinks clink invitingly in carrier bags, and the lucky people chosen to host the party crank their heating up to Caribbean temperatures as the brave revellers of Hollesley get together like penguins for a grand huddle.

How many people can you fit into a fairly small living room dotted generously with side tables decorated with bowls of nuts, crisps and little cheesy pineapple bits on sticks (ok, I made that last one up as a homage to *Abigail's Party*. Might be fun though, anyone got any Demis Roussos tapes?) There is always room for one more person, especially if that person removes several layers of clothing on entering the house. Hence the Caribbean temperature.

I did once try to calculate the optimum guest number by pouring myself a large glass of wine and shuffling round the walls of our living room chanting 'person, drink, person, drink' as Pete noted down the numbers.

However, on the actual party night what you tend to get is 'person, drink, nibbles, handbag (or man-bag), spare cardigan and scarf that the person has removed but can't quite bring themselves to relinquish'. It's getting kinda cosy in here.

Another problem is Nick, who tends to dance.

Put on a Rolling Stones record ('Satisfaction' usually does the trick), clear the floors of breakables if possible stand back and admire a master at work. Pete used to partner him, this is a very fond memory of mine which I hope will in time be repeated.

There was one unforgettable occasion around Christmas a couple of years ago when we were gathered at Danny and Sue's lovely house. Much alcohol had been consumed and the party had reached the stage where everyone was shouting to make themselves heard above the music. Danny and Sue have a very fine and glamorous coffee table, which was tastefully decked with expensive looking festive baubles and tempting finger foods.

However, this didn't stop Nick. As Mick Jagger shook his maracas and bemoaned his inability to find satisfaction, our boules captain leapt onto the table, arms waving and hips grinding. Ray and Gill tried to get him down but it was useless. You can't keep a good man down, and Nick was unstoppable.

By some Christmas miracle nothing was damaged, and someone even managed to video the performance. The temptation to upload it onto YouTube was great, but I'm sure Nick has something equally embarrassing on the rest of us somewhere (probably boules related) so we resisted.

The strange thing about Nick though is the fact that even though he never misses the chance to dance in public if the music is right, when it comes to his own eagerly anticipated Christmas extravaganza, traditionally held on the weekend before Christmas to get us all in the mood, there is no music and no dancing.

But there are rules. I often think that next to moths, sport and the Stones, rules are Nick's favourite things.

These rules are explained to people when they arrive but as they are made by a man who spends the entire party topping up people's glasses, they carry little weight with the revellers.

Rule 1- Do not linger in the kitchen.

As this is where all the booze hangs out, this rule stands no chance at all. Also, as it is small and warm Nick's kitchen is the perfect place to huddle. Given enough mince pies and red wine I would happily spent the whole winter in there.

Rule 2 - Circulate.

Do not hog dark corners gossiping with your closest friend/next door neighbour/partner. Talk to new people.

Rule 3 - Do not sit down.

Yes, well, if you don't want us to sit down Nick you should remove all your big squashy chairs. By midnight half of us are curled up on these like Labradors in front of a blazing fire. Probably next to our best friend/next door neighbour/partner or that lovely new person that Nick introduced you to about three hours ago. Honestly, it can be like Blind Date in there, should I buy a hat?

Rule 4 - Bring food.

We don't need asking, we live in Hollesley!

It's like the Great British Bake Off with the addition of olives and mixed nuts. This year I discovered that someone had made a chocolate Baileys cake. This is the kind of new person I'd really like to meet. I could take them home with me, we've got a spare room if I shift some of the craft stuff.

I have met some very interesting people at Nick's Christmas do's, we have talked politics and religion and Brexit and even sport and moths, but unfortunately I can never remember these conversations or the people I had them with the next day. It's like trying to recall a dream, clutch it and it's gone. I can only hope the other person has the same problem, because I dread to think what I was burbling on about after my fifth glass of red and third slice of chocolate Baileys cake. Thank goodness this only happens once a year.

There has been an interesting new trend recently, in fact an interesting new word 'hygge', a Danish word which seems to translate roughly as 'cosiness', or as I touched on previously in the chapter on Arts and Crafts, a love of all things Kirstie Allsopp.

We're such trendsetters here in Hollesley, we were busy hygge-ing back in 2014 before it became fashionable. In fact I am now tempted to change the title of this chapter to 'hyggering in Hollesley ' but it seems a little pretentious for us simple country folk, as well as sounding a little rude, and anyway huddling is what we do.

I put 'definition of hygge' into Google (sometimes it's a struggle to fill those long winter evenings). Along with pictures of ambitious Nordic knits and snugly blankets, this explanation came up -

> 'The art of building sanctuary and community, of inviting closeness and paying attention to what makes us feel open hearted and alive.
>
> To create well-being, a connection and warmth, a feeling of belonging to the moment and to each other.
>
> Celebrating the everyday.'

There was a lot more in this vein, and instead of cringing at the sentimentality of it all, I wanted to open a bottle of something celebratory and cheer, because let's face it, it's a bloody miracle we're both here to tell this tale at all. Go on, give yourself a treat and Google hygge then go out and buy yourself a hygge book, that's what I'm about to do to celebrate getting out of 2016 alive.

It's been a strange and scary year, but at least we all feel strange and scared together.

I'm just glad we're not famous, although this could change as Pete got his ukulele for Christmas, even as I write I can hear him plinking in the living room. Move over Ed Sheeran, Pete is putting Hollesley on the map. In 2017, just you watch, they'll be selling guided tours of our little villages, the Sorrel Horse will need a bigger car park, and maybe even indoor toilets! You won't be able to get into the Shepherd and Dog for queues of eager autograph hunters begging to hear 'I don't look good naked anymore'.

I think this is now a good point to finish our adventures with the story of a very personal and moving huddle which took place on Shingle Street on the cold and breezy Friday that was Twelfth night, January 6 2017. The very brave and inspiring Mat Bayfield from the Broadside Boys has set himself the challenge of organising a different Walk and Talk around the villages and small towns of Suffolk on each day of January to raise funds for the Brain Tumour Charity. Mat himself was diagnosed with a rare and inoperable brain tumour and underwent extensive treatment at Addenbrooke's hospital. He has responded well to treatment and lives his life to the full, managing to remain so cheerful and positive it gives you hope.

So we decided to join his band of walkers for a 3 to 4 mile hike through the winter fields and along the shingle beach, where we chatted with lots of interesting people, some of whom had their own tales of triumph over adversity to tell. Then we huddled together for a photo shoot before setting off for a cuppa at the nearby Hollesley Bay Prison. This was rather exciting as Mat was unfamiliar with the area and instead of driving to the cafe he led our convoy of around a dozen vehicles into the car-park of the main prison itself, past a sign forbidding entry by the general public!

Somehow we managed to avoid becoming inmates and were guided to the cafe where the guy serving on his own suddenly found himself with the challenge of around two dozen hungry and thirsty walkers crammed into a small space. He coped magnificently.

Fed and watered, we put our hands deeply into our pockets for Mat's charity and began organising the next adventure. Some people aim to do all the walks, so we have promised to come when we can and to think up ideas for more fund –raising along the way. We went home feeling refreshed and upbeat about the future, but that is what this magical place is all about, and it's the reason we're not going anywhere, because we belong here, where everyone knows our name.

Many thanks to:

This section of the book could get rather long as I have so many people to thank and I wouldn't want to leave anyone out, so I have decided to make separate lists. I love a list.

Bookmates …

All my friends and family who have put up with me droning on about this book for the last four years. I'll shut up now.

A special mention to my friend Anne, who said she was so engrossed that reading my book made her late for table tennis. Couldn't ask for higher praise!

Everyone who ploughed through my earlier versions and spotted typos and howlers. Can't believe some of the stuff I thought I could get away with. This kind of thing also helps you grow a very thick skin.

Lifesavers....

Hayley, Simon and Keith. I will always be so grateful you were there.

The East Anglian Air Ambulance, love you guys. But don't want to see you again anytime soon!

The paramedic team who came out on July 23rd, not only totally professional but cheerful and sympathetic too.

Basildon Cardiac Unit, so proud of our wonderful NHS.

Liz and Niall, true friends when I needed them most, nothing was too much trouble, can't thank you enough.

Karrie, your texts in the early hours saved my sanity. They are still on my phone.

Christine, for wine and pretzels and watching the bake-off with me when I had reached rock bottom.

All the villagers who included us in their prayers, someone was listening.

Supporters....

My wonderful son Alister, for putting me up and putting up with me and giving up his holiday. Sorry…

My equally wonderful daughter Helen for always being there and managing to say just the right things at the right time.

All my gorgeous grandchildren for cheering me up, especially Evie for my spa bath.

Nick for helping Pete without having to be asked. I'm sure the two of you will dance again some day.

Boules Friends

All the Bouligans team for the happy memories.

The Thursday Boules Club, you mad bunch of stars.

Sheila from the Parrot for our anniversary meal and cheesy chips.

Music

Eric Sedge of the Broadside Boys for letting me use the words to 'Everyone knows my name'

Mat Bayfield for walking and talking and being such an inspiration. We completed five charity walks, including the magnificent Glemham Hall experience which attracted 540 walkers and made the front page of the East Anglia Daily Times and also a good spot on BBC Look East. Fame at last. At the final count over £20,000 was raised for the Brain Tumour Charity, and more walks are planned.

Lucy and John aka Honey and the Bear, love your gorgeous songs.

Bawdsey John for the harmonicas round my hat day.

Eliza and family for your wonderful talent, makes us proud to live here.

Chris and Carrie for the Sorrel Horse music nights and the penny gaffe.

Bluesy Ray Booth for 'I Don't Look Good Naked Anymore'. As he has now joined Weight Watchers he may have to learn some new songs – 'I'm Too Sexy For My Shirt' perhaps?

In fact, all the places, friends and experiences that have formed our new life over the past five years, for us life began again at sixty-two and we can't wait to see what Suffolk has to throw at us in the years to come. Whatever it is, we'll be ready for it!

Coming soon …

Take a look at the first chapter
from Sue's new book about her
further adventures in East Suffolk

Come in at Random, in any Key

You like

Chapter One

You could say, without fear of contradiction, that the area we have chosen as our home on the Bawdsey Peninsula in East Suffolk is remote. It is also quiet. Large crowds of people are rarely seen, unless you can count crowds of birdwatchers who will arrive en masse at the merest rumour of a rare bird to be captured on film. They're all the same to me, birds, boring brown things that go tweet, but I digress. Noisy crowds are as rare as windless days on Shingle Street, so the night of the Great Real Ale Enthusiasts Invasion of the Swan at Alderton was a night to remember.

It was the evening of 10th March 2017 and a small, discreet band of music fans had gathered in the dark, intimate bar of the Swan in order to support our good friend Kevin's effort to start a local open mic evening. It's not easy to get musicians from more populous areas of Suffolk, such as Snape and Aldeburgh, to come to our 'back of beyond' pubs to perform, so often the open mic just comprises Kevin and his trusty guitar.

Kevin likes to pay tribute to recently dead pop musicians, so you can imagine how he enjoyed the harvest of 2016. David Bowie, George Michael, Prince, Leonard Cohen, none missed his loving renditions of their most popular numbers. We call him the Dead Singer.

Around a dozen of us music lovers had spread ourselves around the bar for a gentle evening's entertainment when suddenly the doors burst open and the carnival began.

Around 27 people (it felt like many more, believe me) burst into the Swan, all talking at once, loudly. I think they may have been drinking.

It transpired that we had been chosen by the Ipswich Real Ale Enthusiasts to be part of a coach trip which was in reality a pub crawl of four Peninsula hostelries. I think we were pub number three.

The Enthusiasts (great name for a band, by the way) came in all shapes and sizes and both sexes, somehow resembling a gathering of life-sized garden gnomes. As crews go they couldn't have been motley-er, some being quite startlingly well-built while others were more your dwarf version. One sported a fetching afro hairstyle straight out of the '70s, I think he may also have been wearing a tank top. They were raucous, rowdy and totally wonderful. We had a party on our hands. They were world class minglers, it was as if we had known them from our own disco dancing days, and the sound of our merrymaking bounced off the walls for around an hour and then suddenly they left, all at once, like a flock of birds startled by a predator.

I think the driver of their minibus had reminded them all that there was one more quiet country pub for them to enliven before closing time put an end to their shenanigans, and so we waved them off like family at Christmas, with cries of 'Safe journey' and 'Come back soon'. And then they were gone, leaving a ringing in the ears and a waft of real ale in the air.

Kevin reached for his guitar again and began to sing, sadly and with much reverence, 'Ground control to Major Tom'.

Dear Reader

If you have enjoyed reading this book,
then please tell your friends and relatives
and leave a review on Amazon.
Thank you.

About the Author

Sue Thompson was born a long, long time ago in Portsmouth. A year later the family moved to Southend in Essex where she remained, somewhat unwillingly, until 2013, when she escaped with her husband to rural Suffolk. Prior to this many happy years were spent working in libraries where she dreamed of adding her own books to the shelves. This is her first book but the bug has bitten deep and two more are now planned. You can follow her progress on Facebook.

https://www.facebook.com/Sue-Thompson-Author-1784360638472543/?pnref=story.unseen-section

Printed by Amazon Italia Logistica S.r.l.
Torrazza Piemonte (TO), Italy

50346675R00080